Happy Volunteers, Happy Nonprofits

The guide to getting and keeping great volunteers.

J Brady

Hello!

This book is for making happy volunteers and happy nonprofits an achievable goal. If you are creating new volunteer programs, we're here to help. If you have volunteer programs that need improvement, we're here to help you too!

This book does not waste your time with fluff or theory. All you need to do is read and do the exercises in each chapter to ensure a successful program.

When people are happy, they feel a sense of responsibility and commitment;

they will give you more than you ask.

Who am I to tell you how to start a program and why did I write a book? The topics discussed in this book are important to me. I have experience with great volunteer programs and also ones that can use some help. I found many of them had the same problems that kept them constantly having to find more volunteers.

What are those nonprofits doing that isn't working? The way nonprofit staff communicates with their volunteers is a big factor in volunteer retention and satisfaction. Volunteers do not sign up consistently if they feel they are not valued, or they do not feel like they are making a difference. If they aren't valued or aren't making a difference, why would they bother?

The best programs I helped manage consisted of many volunteers who maintained a regular schedule for years. It was impressive to see how loyal they were, and it became clear that the organization treated them just as kindly.

✳ Getting talented volunteers to stay with your nonprofit requires a strategy.

What makes volunteers great?

(It's not just the free labor.)

- They are the best word of mouth.

- They are great testimonials of your work.

- Great testimonials mean more funding.

- They come to special events.

- They invite friends who become fans.

- They bring innovative ideas and see things from the public's perspective, which is great feedback for you.

- The fact that they work for free speaks volumes about how great your organization is.
- They save millions of dollars a year!

Volunteering is as rewarding for the volunteers as it is for those they serve.

A little about communication:

It is important to start off on the right foot.

Be sure volunteers know their role and expectations within the first interview and orientation.

Make them confident that they will get a great experience working with you.

Listen to what they want from you and then give them great instructions so they know what you want from them.

Be willing to welcome new ideas. I have worked with many nonprofits that do not value feedback from volunteers. This is not helpful. With many advisors, we find success. Let volunteers be creative and even learn new skills or use their professional experience. Give them confidence by considering their suggestions. Weigh if their suggestions are a good return on your investment and if they work with your mission statement.

How to politely disagree: If you don't like a volunteer's suggestion, let them know nicely why it does not work. Be sure volunteers know that you want to continue talking to them about ideas that might make their suggestion work in the future.

Creating confidence: You don't want to give "busy work" to someone who is motivated to learn. Allow creativity to flourish even in the most basic tasks. Let them know how their work makes a different.

Define Your Needs

Before defining our volunteer needs, be sure you have everything you need as a new nonprofit. Since this is your passion, you need to do it right.

Before you recruit:

- Create your board of directors

- Write your vision and mission statements

- Establish bylaws and policies

- Become tax exempt (becoming tax exempt gets you more donations)

- Check that you are meeting all requirements for your state's standards

Once you have all those, we can think more about recruiting volunteers. Alright, now let's get to volunteering.

What Kind of Volunteers Do You Need for Your Nonprofit?

Each person is blessed with a unique gift.

Labor Volunteers

If you provide a service to others, you have probably thought of the value of "labor volunteers." If you are an animal shelter, they foster and feed animals. If you are a gift shop, they are the sales staff. If you deliver food to hungry seniors, they pack the food and make deliveries. They feed the hungry, teach seniors, socialize animals, clean gutters, garden, and much more!

Labor volunteers do work that relates to the mission statement of the nonprofit. It is hands-on and rewarding. I won't go into this as much as the other opportunities because they will vary by the organization.

If you use expert professionals for labor positions, they might be paid staff. For example, nurses and veterinarians typically work for an affordable price.

Now let us look at the many volunteer position types that every nonprofit needs.

Office Staff

Provide the administrative functions of the office. Many times you will see a founder try to do everything when they start. If your nonprofit is expanding in size and services, you need a volunteer coordinator, a receptionist, and a manager. This can consist of a group of volunteers doing each position, or one or two paid staff members to do all of it.

Paid or volunteer, you're going to need people who can work flexible hours. They'll need to exude professionalism. They should be good at problem solving and must be passionate about your organization!

A **volunteer coordinator** provides orientations, creates schedules, interviews volunteers, reviews applications, and manages volunteers.

A **receptionist** is the face and voice of your nonprofit when the public contacts you or comes to you. Their personality needs to be genuinely friendly because they represent your NPO.

A **manager** ensures that everything is working smoothly. They know what office supplies you need, what the schedule is, and if you have enough volunteers. They know how your organization works. This opportunity is stressful and is not very glamorous.

Website volunteers. All computer-related volunteer opportunities are important. They save a lot of money and create your brand. Most people hear about a nonprofit through their website and social media!

Website developer and designer. You'll need someone to design and manage your website. Be sure to review volunteer applicant's portfolio to be sure you like their style.

A **social media volunteer** updates your social networks and keeps your fans interested and engaged. This is how people hear about your work, your special events, and how to donate money. To be successful, you need to have computer-savvy people helping you.

Creative Volunteers

A **graphic designer** will need to design/refine your logo. This logo is used for your website, t-shirts, business cards, and more.

Videographers are great to enhance your mission for your YouTube account and social networks.

Photographers are important for Instagram, social networking, flyers, and more.

Writers write website content, newsletter emails, and blogs.

Fundraising Volunteers

As much as we don't enjoy asking for money, it's what keeps the nonprofit in business. This means you are going to need a stellar group for fundraising.

This includes:

An **event planner** to coordinate all fundraising and volunteer thank you events.

A **grant writer** to write for you when you apply to grants, this volunteer will also need to be good at the research needed to find grants.

Public relations volunteers or staff get you in good with the public.

Some of the staff might be paid because it is worth investing in them to get you more donations. With regular donations you can focus on doing good work.

The "All-Volunteer" Concept

Some nonprofits like to say "Every bit of your donations go to (insert cause: the animals, etc.)" "All-volunteer" programs sound good; but does saying this convince more people to donate? Are you being your most efficient by not paying anyone as staff?

Most importantly, your organization needs to be a 501(c)(3) so that those who donate can write off donations on their taxes. That is gets people see you as a real nonprofit. That, and feeling that donations make a difference (see a theme?) Thank those who support you in every way (both big and small donations.) Being transparent with your funds also makes people trust you when they donate money.

Should Some Positions Be Paid?

It is better to have some paid opportunities, but only if it is within your budget. If you're blessed with talented and professional volunteers, that's awesome! If you need paid staff, but cannot afford them, consider **contract work** for projects.

Some paid staff might include:

Event planners

Development professionals (grant writers)

Full-time Administrative Assistant (can be a manager/volunteer coordinator/receptionist)

Accountants

Many Nonprofits Hire Part-time Staff

Be mindful that people who work part-time might eventually want full-time. Providing a good hourly pay will attract people with professional experience. What kinds of people might want to work part-time?

New graduates who need experience: They will want to be full-time eventually, but like learning and want to do great work.

People who are changing careers: Eventually they will also want to be full-time, but will want to learn all about the work.

Students: Happy to work part-time, students will have to work around school hours. When they graduate they need full-time work.

Stay at home parents: If this meets their income needs, this can be a great situation for you and them.

Retirees: Can be a great fit if you meet their income needs.

Internships are a great solution and can be non-paid, paid, or provide school credit. All internship guidelines need to be researched. Some professions have internship requirements that you have to follow, some states might have different rules. Interns are motivated and innovative. Be sure to offer a good letter of recommendation.

Exercise: Create a list of your needs and how many volunteers you need. Are any paid?

Advertise Opportunities

When writing advertisements ask yourself,

"Would I want to volunteer here?"

On a quick note, your best forms of advertising are published stories about your organization. You can get volunteers, donations, and more by advertising this way.

Writing an advertisement the easy way: Have a basic template you can plug opportunities into for each volunteer:

   Title: Have a title that is SEO friendly. This means it includes the words people will use to search for this kind of opportunity.

   Introduction: Start with a question that gets people interested and lets them know the issue you care about.

Information: Let people know the solution to the issue and how their talents can help. Do not sound desperate; you want to sound organized and enthusiastic. Tell them what makes volunteering with you great.

Contact: Have a call to action with contact information. For example: "Email us today!"

Where do I advertise? You can advertise many places for different kinds of volunteers. Use this guide to find what you need.

Students and interns: Coffee shops, Facebook, Twitter. Talk to high schools or colleges about how they advertise volunteer opportunities.

Retirees: Senior centers, senior apartments, AARP website. There are plenty of seniors who use the internet too!

The public: Volunteer websites, flyers, social media.

Sample ads: See this example of an advertisement for a labor position that does everything we have suggested.

Stellar Cat Foster Parents. Love what you do.

Do you love animals? There is a large population of homeless pets in Florida. The Loving Animal Club is a 501(c)(3) nonprofit in Tampa, FL. Our mission is to create loving homes for needy pets. These animals enrich the lives of their people!

*Come join our volunteer team. You **CAN** improve the life of a pet in need! We need foster care volunteers to give our animals their time and affection so they can be socialized for their furever homes.*

In addition to the warm fuzzy feeling of caring for an animal, our volunteers enjoy many social perks. We are an enthusiastic network of foster fur parents. This includes pizza parties, insider rescue newsletters, discounts on merchandise and of course, friendship!

Will you join us? Contact us today for an application.

Spacing is important because it makes everything easier to read. Put new ideas in each paragraph.

Have other people read your ad and provide feedback. You are telling people why they want to volunteer for you (like a commercial for an awesome nonprofit!). In each advertisement, include your mission statement and any perks of working with you.

Now see this ad and how we worked with our template to advertise for *paid* work:

Part-time Veterinarian for Tampa, FL Rescue. Love what you do.

Do you love animals? There is a large population of homeless pets in Florida. The Loving Animal Club is a 501(c)3 nonprofit in Tampa, FL. Our mission is to create loving homes for needy pets. These animals enrich the lives of their people.

Come join our team as a part-time veterinarian to give care to our animals as we achieve our goal of reducing homeless pets. You can improve the life of a pet in need! We need an enthusiastic DVM who can perform spay/neuters, basic exams, vaccinations, and surgery.

Your work will be rewarding and interesting as you meet new animals getting ready for their forever homes!

In addition to the rewards of being a rescue staff, we offer a complete benefit package including health insurance, professional dues, and continuing education.

You are also invited to the same perks as our volunteers. This includes pizza parties, insider rescue newsletters, discounts on merchandise, and friendship!

Contact us today for an application.

Paper flyers are still important. Most of your advertising will be online, but you also should advertise with flyers in some places. You can use the same template as your online advertisements, but you'll need to make sure that it is interesting. This type of advertising will attract those who might not have thought of volunteering, but get interested when they are educated about your cause.

Things to include on flyers:

- A colorful, interesting photo

- Font that is large enough to read

- Your mission statement and name of your NPO

- Include contact information! Very important!

Exercises: Create a list of where you want to advertise. Write a sample ad template. Create a flyer. Be sure you have applications for when people apply.

Interview Applicants

Each volunteer is representative of your nonprofit.

Review applications and contact applicants. There are many people who want to volunteer. There are some things to know about the personalities of people that might come to work with you. This is to give you an idea of things to consider to keep you and your volunteers happy.

Students: High school and college students are likely ready to learn and ambitious. Their schedule might be busy, but they hope to find experience in working with you. They might have ideas that are new.

Retirees: There is a large pool of new retirees. Many find that although they are retired, they need to keep busy and give back. How great is that? They come with years of professional experience and a flexible schedule.

The public: They are passionate about what you are doing and are ready to help you in their free time. They can be experienced professionals and might need a consistent schedule.

Miscellaneous: This includes a segment of the pool who need community service hours, corporate volunteers, and other service days as an option for volunteering. This can be a great fit when you have a project that needs a lot of help.

You'll find that some kinds of people meet your needs more than others for different roles, but everyone has something they can offer.

Overall, there are some main personality traits you'll need to work well together:

- Passion about the work your nonprofit is doing.

- A genuinely upbeat and energetic personality.

- A "get it done" attitude.

- A team player who can work with others and is flexible to new ideas.

Applications: Be sure to contact people who apply to you with an email to let them know you will contact them.

Example:

Hello _____,

Thank you for applying to the _____, we will contact you soon to set up a volunteer interview (or orientation)!

We sincerely appreciate you,

Kittens Bosslady

Put a Volunteer Interests Questionnaire on your Volunteer Application. This is designed to get information about what talents your applicant has and what interests them in this opportunity.

Example Volunteer Interests Questionnaire:

What brings you to (insert nonprofit name)?

What would you like to volunteer doing?

What are you passionate about?

Do you have any volunteer experience?

What hours can you volunteer?

What experience do you want from this opportunity?

Interviewing and asking good questions. A good interview is more like a conversation. Balance this conversation with a great sales pitch for what your nonprofit does. Let your enthusiasm for your work shine through! Your excitement will get others interested.

Your first impression is very important. It is important that you are a friendly, organized, and easy to understand. Communicate your needs and explain your nonprofit's mission, history, and how you work.

Here are some example questions:

- Why do you want to volunteer with us?

- Tell me about yourself.

- Have you volunteered before? How was that?

- Describe a time you worked with someone with whom you did not get along, how did you work on this?

- How do you feel about working with people whom work differently from you?

- How comfortable do you feel working with _____? (Insert population you serve.)

- How comfortable do you feel voicing any questions or complaints? This is where you explain how you are there for any communication needs.

There are many questions you can ask that are specific to your nonprofit. The ones in this book are some examples of general ways to get to know your volunteers.

Once you are happy with your interview, contact the candidate to welcome them and schedule an orientation.

Exercise: Create your interview questions and welcome email.

Teach/Mentor

They need to know how to work.

Orientations are important. A great orientation has a few basics:

- Introduces history of the nonprofit.

- Explains the mission statement and how all your volunteers fulfill this.

- Reads and provides the volunteer manual and has candidates sign an agreement saying they read it and agree to comply.

- Gives a tour and a "how to session" with a mentor.

What's in a Manual?

Basic information about your nonprofit needs to be in your Volunteer Manual:

- The mission statement and how volunteers are helping you achieve your goals.

- Contact information of the volunteer coordinator.

- Volunteer rules.

- Information about creating a schedule that works for everyone.

- Information about signing in hours (because this is very important for taxes).

- Forms your attorney/insurance says you need.

- Explanation of boundaries. For example, they can't ask for money or advertise without your permission.

A great mentor can help keep more volunteers. A mentor needs to be friendly and knowledgeable about your organization. The mentor says good things about your nonprofit. The mentor needs to communicate with you regularly.

Always let everyone in your nonprofit know that they can talk to you and answer their questions. I suggest that you have a suggestion box!

Welcome emails keep people interested. Make sure that you get everyone's emails and check in with them a month after volunteering. You want to ensure that they are happy and that they continue to volunteer with you. Staying in touch makes them feel part of the team and also makes him feel appreciated!

Example welcome letter:

Hello _____,

I am happy to say we at Save the Pets Animal Rescue would like to thank you for becoming a volunteer as a _____!

Our mission to save all the pets in Tampa, FL is a success because of volunteers like you. With your help, we can continue to give great homes to animals who need them. Your donation of time fostering the animals means a lot to us.

Thank you again, and welcome. Please know you can always contact us with any questions.

Sincerely,

Kittens Bosslady

Volunteer Coordinator

Save the Pets Animal Rescue

Exercise: Create your orientation and decide who can mentor new volunteers.

Keep Volunteers Happy

Happy volunteers means MORE volunteers!

Discounts and freebies are a great way to thank people.
Discounts on special events, t-shirts, and more are appreciated
and work as an advertisement too. T-shirts are great advertising.
Some things can even be free to volunteers if it's within your
budget.

Volunteer parties help maintain friendships. Have parties
twice a year to show your appreciation for your volunteers. They
don't have to be expensive if you can't afford to do them: You
can have a pizza party, or even just a pot luck. The point is that
you need to put forth the effort to show your gratitude and to

create friendships. Volunteers have the same goals as each other. It is great to get together to celebrate your common interest.

Volunteer birthdays are a great opportunity to communicate and celebrate. Small volunteer programs are encouraged to celebrate with things like a potluck lunch. Bigger nonprofits can send a personal card to show their thanks. When your volunteers sign up, note their birthday in a calendar.

Email newsletters should already be part of your communication with your sponsors and donators. Have an exclusive volunteer email newsletter that highlights goals you have achieved and "need to know" information. This will remind them about why they volunteered with you. This lets them know that they truly make a difference! Try to email every 6 weeks, or more, if you have great content.

Ideas to write about in your newsletters:

- FAQ's

- Surveys

- Spotlight on someone you're helping (if they agree)

- Special events

- Thank you's to volunteers and funders.

The email address that your email comes from needs to be professional with your nonprofit name in the address.

Thank you's mean a lot. If a volunteer truly goes above and beyond to help you, send them a personalized thank you. Who should you send them to?

- Someone who took extra time to help volunteer in the schedule while someone is on maternity leave.

- Someone who did a lot of lifting or helped your nonprofit move.

- Someone who helped you receive a lot of donations via social media.

"Bring-a-Friend" Day is going to be your new favorite thing. Ask volunteers to invite a friend to volunteer or for a tour. Be sure that they sign any agreements/waivers needed. This is fun for them and will get you more fans and more volunteers.

Volunteer surveys are important. A good nonprofit should always ask themselves "How can we improve?" We talked about a volunteer questionnaire; now another important concept is a volunteer feedback survey. The point of this is to emphasize that they can tell you about their suggestions (you did create that suggestion box, right?). Like everything in regular life, communication is important.

Communicate kindly. We've included some phrases to say often:

"Great idea!"

"You did a great job!"

"Thank you for coming in!"

"This looks great!"

"Thank you for helping us _____ when you _____."

"We're glad you are here!"

There are also phrases not to say:

"You're wrong."

Instead try saying: "Let me show you how.. or a way that has worked for us is…"

"Stop complaining. Don't complain to other volunteers."

Instead try saying: "How can we solve this problem? Please know we are open to talking about this and resolving these issues. What can we do to help?"

Exercise: Create 3 ideas for volunteer celebrations.

CONGRATS!

You've learned the basics to great volunteering.

You know what makes great volunteers.

You know you have to know what you need.

You know how to write a great advertisement to hire passionate people.

You know you NEED to interview and mentor staff.

You know that you need to balance busy work with creative ideas.

You know keeping volunteers interested requires making them feel appreciated!

If you ever have any questions or need consulting please contact us at NonprofitKitten@Gmail.com, we are happy to help. Thank you for reading!

Printed in Great Britain
by Amazon